DRAW IT WITH ME: **THE**
ELEGANT
FEMALE FORM

An Intimate Study of the Beautiful Feminine
Figure in Varied Chic & Classical Poses

DRAW IT WITH ME: THE
ELEGANT
FEMALE FORM

*An Intimate Study of the Beautiful Feminine
Figure in Varied Chic & Classical Poses*

BRIAN C HAILES

Presented by Epic Edge Publishing™
in cooperation with Draw It With Me™

Draw It With Me - The Elegant Female Form: An Intimate Study of the Beautiful Feminine Figure in Varied Chic & Classical Poses © 2023 Brian C Hailes

This is an Epic Edge Publishing, LLC, publication
In cooperation with Draw It With Me™
First edition, published 2023

Printed in the USA

Epic Edge Publishing
1934 Fielding Hill Ln,
Draper, UT 84020

All rights reserved. No part of this publication may be reproduced, stored in a retrieval system, or transmitted, in any form or by any means, electronic, mechanical, photocopying, recording, or otherwise, without the prior permission of the copyright holder(s).

Created and produced by Epic Edge Publishing
in cooperation with Draw It With Me
https://www.epicedgepublishing.com
https://www.drawitwithme.com
https://www.youtube.com/drawitwithme
https://www.hailesart.com

Designed and typeset by Epic Edge Publishing, LLC

Written & Illustrated by Brian C Hailes
Cover art by Brian C Hailes

Paperback Edition ISBN: 978-1-951374-76-1
Hardback Edition ISBN: 978-1-951374-75-4
Ebook Edition ISBN: 978-1-951374-77-8

Description: Draw It With Me - The Elegant Female Form: An Intimate Study of the Beautiful Feminine Figure in Varied Chic & Classical Poses art book explores the process of capturing the beautiful female figure in life drawing and in-depth studies of the human form in standing, seated, reclining, kneeling, bending, crouching and other varied poses. Offering step-by-step visual examples and limited process descriptions, this book will provide both aspiring and seasoned artists with a literary and fully illustrated helpmeet designed to inspire and enlighten.

With over 200 full color pages by award-winning artist and bestselling author, Brian C Hailes, this book features artwork of the female form accomplished in pencil, charcoal, watercolor, ink, acrylic, oils and other mixed media with many photo references of the models also included. This exciting and educational reference book will assist in improving your own figure drawing clout and offers many new technical ideas for you to try. It will also help raise your sensitivity to and appreciation for the gorgeous, charming, strong and divine creation that is woman! So pick up your pencil, charcoal, pen or brush, and "Draw It With Me!"

Epic Edge Publishing, LLC
Draw It With Me™

Instagram: @drawitwithmeofficial
Facebook: drawitwithme
ArtStation: bchailes
Original art & prints may be purchased at:
https://www.hailesart.com

This book is dedicated to our faithful customers, followers & subscribers. Thank you for your support!

—B.C. Hailes

CONTENTS

INTRODUCTION

"To the Rescue," 11 x 14 in., Graphite, Color Pencil & Acrylic on Bristol Board

ARTIST'S NOTE

With my first two books on rendering the human form, *Draw It With Me: The Dynamic Female Figure* and *DIWM: A Study of the Human Form*, I set out to continue my own learning process as well as improve my own artistic skills within the confines of figurative artworks. With this third book in the series, these goals remain in effect, but I'm also inclined to introduce other mediums, and develop many of the sketched out pieces further through to completion. Color, style and design are also important factors in figurative art, and as before, this project has given me an excuse to spend more time focused on the subject than I might otherwise have the opportunity to be.

Without delving too deeply in a simple introduction, I feel inclined to ask the question: What is it that separates the hundreds or perhaps thousands of master figurative artists across the world from the millions that merely dabble or struggle to capture correct proportion, line quality, adept use of shadow and light, anatomical mastery, texture, composition, balance or concept brilliance, etc.? What is it that separates the *amateurs* from the *professionals*, so to speak? Or in the gallery space, *those that sell* from *those that don't* (politics and market quirkiness aside)?

In my experience, I've learned that great artists are perhaps like your favorite stage magicians in the sense that upon viewing their captivating tricks, one might jump to the assumption that they were achieved relatively quickly and with a certain ease. However, in truth, the illusion is in play; what might seem fast and easy upon first glance was likely achieved through many hours of planning and construction, schooling, try-fail cycles, frustration, experimentation, near failure or abandonment and ultimately . . . *finally* . . . success.

Many of the masters of old would spend years on a given piece, either propped up by their financial patrons or living in poverty to achieve the quality we see in some of our museums.

Years on a piece. Just think of it. In our society bathed in *bigger, better, faster, more*, few there are that take the time to not only smell, but *paint* the roses or, like the ancient samurai, to focus on developing one and only one skill for a lifetime sans the distractions of streaming television, social media and endless entertainment options. Perhaps the all-prevalent *consumer* assimilates us all while the more rare *producer* goes the way of the dodo (or computer AI). But to spend years on a piece, staring at the same composition, to me, seems a near impossible task (unless, of course, one has twenty works in progress that they juggle on 'musical easels,' *which I do . . . shhh*).

How does one compete? First of all, just because one magician can pull a rabbit out of a hat doesn't mean it's not impressive when another does the same, or perhaps with a new spin.

We artists can be hard on ourselves. I'm always giving myself impossible deadlines. Unrighteous expectations. Unnecessary stress. What if I'm not making enough? What's enough? Millions? Six figures? Sufficient for my family's needs? Artists are rarely known for the money they make. Yet one can make a splash. But is that what it's about, if not money? Making a splash? If I never produce another work of art, will anyone care? Has anyone even seen the works I've already done? Does anyone *like* them? Enough to pull out their wallets? Could I do it again? Was the output worth the input? The list goes on, and these are questions we all must face.

Yes, you may ask, but what has all this to do with figure art? Figurative art, as with any art form has a faceless enemy, and that enemy is distraction. Distraction from what?

Practice.

An artist must put practice into her art, just as a surgeon must practice his surgical skills. And if one gets too busy or caught up thinking of money, fame, vacations, the possibility of failure, a new TV series they might be missing, or any number of probable interruptions, one can quite easily become a nonstarter. Then who puts on the magic show?

In other words, it's about *becoming*.

When one is drawing from life or putting down strokes on a painting, perhaps listening to great music, and one is in 'the zone,' a simple comment or question from a friend, the vibration of your phone or "Dinner is ready!" is all it takes to break the progression.

I'm not saying we shouldn't eat supper or reply to our friends' comments, but I am saying it will take a more concerted effort on our part to achieve improvement in today's smartphone-addicted world. Because the hours of practice are still—after all this time and despite all our technological advancements—a necessity.

Apply the *10,000 Hour Rule*, and then, once you've spent that time, double it. Or better yet, don't worry about the timer, and that will give you even more time to draw and paint.

And what better subject to start on than . . . the timeless, beautiful, elegant *human figure*?

—*B.C. Hailes*

STANDING POSES

"Juliet's Window," 9 x 12 in., Color Pencil & Acrylic on Watercolor Board   13

STANDING POSES
RED GYPSY

Color Pencil & Acrylic on Bristol Board
11 x 14 in.

With Tuskan red color pencil, I begin the light sketch (1) with some landmark indication lines, focusing on relation of shapes and overall figure proportion. Then, studying the reference closely, I develop the major shapes and details with careful accuracy. However, I do make a few noticable changes, such as lengthening the thighs and calves, exaggerating the curvature of the torso, hair, and legs as well as the outer drapery lines, and pushing the juxtaposition of darks and lights to give the gypsy girl some added energy and presence. I also loosely and playfully 'scribble' out some spirit lines around the chosen contours to give it a flare of frolic.

From here (2), I attentively drop in those shadows and edge refinements even deeper and develop the surroundings of couch, wall and floor, and introduce a little paint to splash in that vibrant rose red Arabic style bedlah, and make the overall piece generally feel a bit more wet, free and finished.

1

2

3

STANDING POSES
TWINS

Ink & Acrylic on Illustration Board
12 x 16 in.

Sometimes it's fun to combine different reference of the same model into one cohesive piece. At first pass, I was planning for this to be a sort of 'stocato' style black and white artwork done only using ink, but as I produced the drawing, I kept being drawn to those powerful purples and vibrant oranges in the backdrop, floor, wardrobe, and stand, so I absolutely had to apply the added dimension of color to try and mimic that appeal.

In the beginning stages, one must be extremely careful when drawing with ink, as it becomes much like carving in stone. One wrong move and you can disfigure the figure's beauty beyond repair. However, don't let this stop you from trying out the medium. With a little practice, you can start to determine what areas require surgeon-like focus, and which areas you can relax and even play with. I began with 003 0.15mm fineliner micro-pens and increased thickness up to 05 0.45mm ink tips upon completion, going back and forth between sizes as needed, reserving the thicker lines for shadow areas. Attempting to nail the proportional relationship of the figures with one another became the other major challenge, but overall, it seems to have turned out all right. They are twins after all. They get each other.

Photographs © by Brian C Hailes
Model: Lauren Hunsaker

1

2

3

"Just a Girl," 9 x 12 in., Color Pencil on Pastel Toned Paper   17

STANDING POSES
WALK ON THE BEACH

Graphite, Color Pencil & Acrylic on Illustration Board
15 x 20 in.

This piece was done as part of my *Maidens & Monsters* series, and the process videos for both the drawing and painting are available at DrawItWithMe.com and on our "Draw It With Me" YouTube channel.

This was a fun subject matter to tackle in all of its splendid simplicity. All that space and big sky anyone who's ever been to the beach has experienced. The light sand, turquoise water and azure expanse beckons to be enjoyed, and certainly not rushed. This beachside beauty with her . . . dog. Demon dog? Pint-sized four-legged adolescent dragon friend? We'll just stick to *maiden* with her pet *monster*. They seem to be enjoying themselves. Wouldn't you? Perhaps they're just out on a morning walk. Or searching the endless waves for an incoming vessel with precious cargo. Either way, I probably had more fun painting this one than they're having on their leisurely stroll.

STANDING POSES
THE BATHER

Graphite, Color Pencil & Acrylic on Mixed Media Board
12 x 16 in.

In steps 1 and 2, we work in the basic contour shapes softly in graphite, giving ourselves a gentle framework to develop later on. In step 3, we drop in the beginnings of chiaroscuro delicately identifying areas of light and shadow.

To help support the quiet, placid and relaxed mood of the pose, I'm careful to keep the edges soft as we move into the finish work and introduce watered down layers of paint, mindful of the direct light source from the upper right corner of the picture plane, and softly cast shadows down and to the left.

For color temperature on The Bather, I thought it might be nice to give the warmer tones to the girl and let the surroundings cool off into neutral shades of gray. So I focus most of the warm, mindful render work on the center of the figure and loosen up toward the outer edges and background area, giving the majority of thought to the woman standing in the towel, preparing for her bath.

1

2

3

STANDING POSES
DRAGON TRAIL

Graphite, Color Pencil & Acrylic on
Illustration Board
15 x 20 in.

STANDING POSES
REMEMBRANCE

Graphite & Color Pencil on Mixed Media Board
12 x 16 in.

Old vintage photos can make wonderful reference for figurative works as they hold a special historical air about them. Even photos taken by unknown or unrecorded photographers from the distant past. The hairstyles, the film quality, the melodramatic poses and theatrical lighting . . . It all just begs to be drawn.

Starting with swift, flitting gestural lines to flesh out the form, we try and evoke the feeling of the work, not just the technical rendering. Of course, there is something to be said for adept and skillful render work, as well as having a keen eye for anatomical, compositional or proportional problems to be solved throughout each step of the journey, but the piece should also have some heart. The lines, the angles, the longing—we attempt to encapsulate some emotion underneath all the systematic line placement and shading work. At the end of the day, if the piece doesn't make you *feel* anything, then the artist has failed indeed.

1

2

3

STANDING POSES
A WITCH'S DISPOSITION

Graphite, Color Pencil & Acrylic on Illustration Board
12 x 16 in.

Begin with gesture that informs the general feel of the pose and specifies the broad shapes, giving a comfortable framework on which to build (1) as you continue to study your reference and refine the accord between those shapes and shadows (2). And then continue the journey to deepen those relationships between dark and light, playing with the textures, focus and chiaroscuro to bring it to the finished drawing (3), and ultimately apply color in paint (4). Having a vague idea in mind for the finished product, such as dropping a flat mauve or violet into the background can inspire enjoyable experimentation with style and media. But often, that initial idea can morph into something new at each step until your piece becomes very different from your original vision.

As opposed to a witch's evil disposition for her tendency to constantly give in to the Devil's influence, an artist must fight the urge to make everything look the same.

1

2

3

4

STANDING POSES
A STUDY OF THE HUMAN FORM

Graphite & Color Pencil on Toned Paper
9.4 x 12.2 in.

Originally created for the wraparound cover of my second figure book entitled, *Draw It With Me: A Study of the Human Form*, I wanted to showcase both the male and female forms in a tasteful yet evocative manner, giving the illustration a classical feel while also bringing it into the 21st century.

Using light pencil marks up front is important so as to keep the process fluid and any mistakes, easily editable. Some 'purist' artists don't use erasers, and let the outcome simply happen as it will, mistakes and all, and I do approach some pieces that way, but when you have it in the back of your mind that this particular work will ultimately be a cover (and you don't want to do it three or four times start to finish), a little light erasure work can be helpful at each pass. Varying the dark and light tones in the background around each figure can also add to the visual appeal and give even the most static areas some added tension and energy. Having the figures turned away from one another also helps with a different kind of tension . . . the *sexual* kind.

1

2

3

STANDING POSES
LITHE FIGURE

Graphite, Color Pencil, Watercolor & Acrylic on Mixed
Media Board
12 x 16 in.

Keeping a piece expressive and remisiscent is often my
greatest objective while developing an artwork; truly,
energy is the name of the game. Efficiency and accuracy
obviously matter to some (like myself) more than to
others, however, the intensity of one's reaction or response
becomes *more*—or at least *as*—important.

This piece from concept to completion felt as though
it needed to be *raw, fiery, vulnerable,* thus the warm red,
ochre and sienna tones. The fleshy backdrop also assists in
giving the overall quality an earthy or 'grunge' type feeling.
I like to juxtapose the smooth, soft, sometimes shiny
textures of the skin with much grittier or harsher paint/
pencil strokes. I suppose in a way this is to emphasize the
human condition. We are, after all, delicate and fragile
beings experiencing life in often coarse and dangerous
environments or circumstances. And how much control
do we actually have?

1

2

3

4

STANDING POSES
FENCES CAN ALSO BE PRISONS

Graphite on Mixed Media Board
12 x 16 in.

It's all in the eyes . . . While this phrase has been overused nearly to the point of becoming a cliche', there's obviously something to it. The eyes can reveal a lot about one's inner state and emotions. Perhaps not everyone has gazed into another's eyes for the first time, and felt like they had known them forever, but it's surely true that the eyes are the windows to the soul. So it then becomes important to draw them well and in the right place.

A straightforward drawing, *Fences Can Also Be Prisons* refers to the often standoffish approach we imbue into our relationships—much like practice for an artist. We put up our walls, we set up unrealistic boundaries—as a defensive mechanism, perhaps, or because of a system of beliefs. We play games, pretend we're not interested, don't give credit where credit is due, hold each other at arms length or more. But we must remember that when all is said and done, united we stand, divided we fall, and the fences we put up can also become prisons.

1

2

3

LIFE DRAWING STUDIES

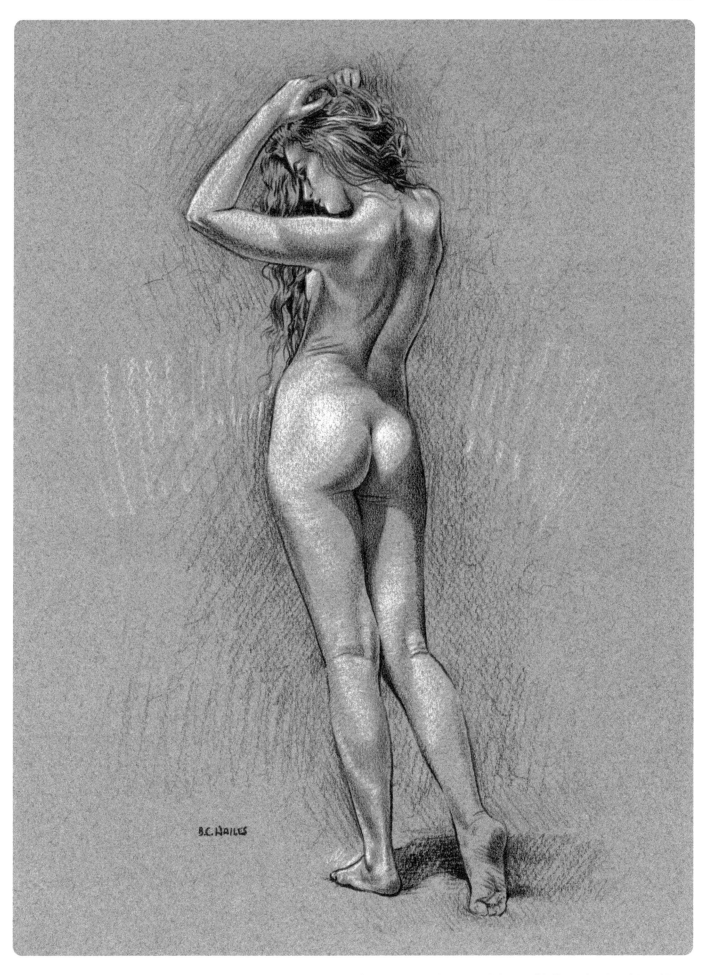

STANDING POSES
GESTURES & 30–45 MINUTE SKETCHES

Gesture drawing is a type of life drawing that prioritizes flowing movement, resulting in sketchy, fluid lines with less defined shapes than contour drawing, and often takes around 2 to 5 minutes. Most gestural drawings utilize the human figure as the subject, making it a type of figure drawing. (Most of the examples shown in this spread are scattered across the bottom of the page below and opposite. They are the more simplistic, less involved pieces. The more 'finished' sketches shown are the result of more careful execution and furthering of the form, shading and detail in chiaroscuro (toward the top & middle of the spread). Most of these were achieved in about 30 to 45 minutes from start to completion, give or take.

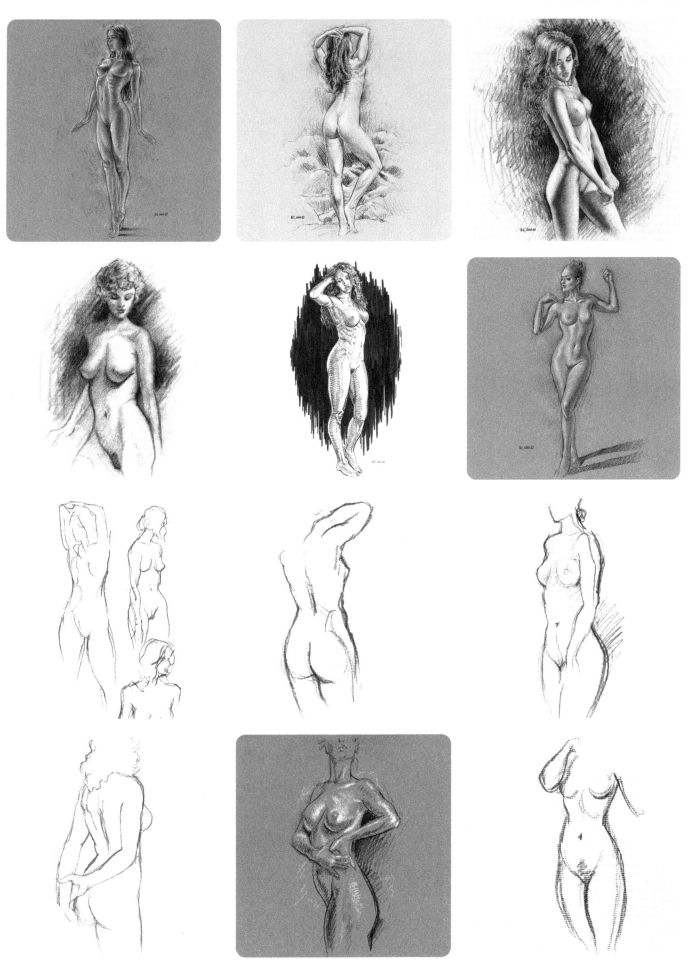

SEATED POSES

"An Elegant Back," 9.4 x 12.2 in., Charcoal & Nupastel on Toned Paper

SEATED POSES
EVE

Graphite, Color Pencil, Watercolor & Acrylic on Canson
Mixed Media Artboard
16 x 12 in.

*"I gasp, and I'm Eve in the Garden of Eden, and he's the
serpent, and I cannot resist."*

—E.L. James

This particular piece was done with the above quotation
in mind using the below reference photo and also my
imagination for the background vegetation as a sort of
spot illustration intended for use in an upcoming book
entitled, "Maidens & Monsters."

It was also an experiment in mixed media as it utilizes the
strengths of several different mediums as indicated above.
Laying in layer after layer, each time switching out your
tools and swapping graphite pencil for oil-based colored
pencil, and oil-based pencil for brush can be an enjoyable
and liberating exercise. Somehow, knowing you're going
to be making another pass using a different set of utensils
can boost your confidence as you work . . . right up until
that next stage actually begins.

1

2

3

4

SEATED POSES
ONLY INSECURITIES

Graphite & Color Pencil on Hahnemuhle Ingres Paper
9.4 x 12.2 in.

A piece done specifically to grace the back cover of this particular book, *Only Insecurities* was a practice in careful and delicate precision. It's an enjoyable challenge to engage in different approaches to varying projects, some renderd with loose and energetic experimentation, some tightly rendered and softly caressed to a polished finish. Or some that reside in a space in between.

Gestural lines carefully placed and flowing to give the idea of the major forms gives us a basic ghost of a figure to build upon (1). More details in contour flesh her out, down to even locks of hair, pupils, and wrinkles in the pointed feet (2). Moving on from light marks in graphite to noir (black) Color Pencil to enhance the shadows in chiaroscuro, we carve out the angelic three-dimensional form with something like subtle hatch marks that move around the softly curving structures of the naked body (3). Attention is liberally given to the feeling conveyed through the eyes of the model, and cool colors are introduced to give totality to the vulnerable figure (4).

1

2

3

4

1

2

3

4

"Alone in the Grass," 12 x 16 in., Graphite, Color Pencil & Acrylic on Watercolor Board

1

2

3

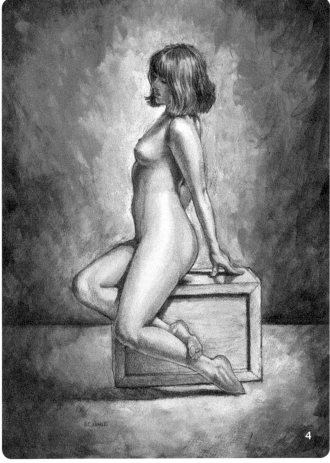

4

"Edge of the Box," 12 x 16 in., Graphite, Color Pencil & Acrylic on Watercolor Board   45

SEATED POSES
GREEK GODDESS

Graphite & Color Pencil on Toned Paper
9.4 x 12.2 in.

I have always been drawn to the classical figure that appears throughout sculpture, paintings, and architecture from the Greek and Roman empires as well as other northeastern Mediterranean civilizations existing even long before the Dark Ages of the 12th–9th centuries BC and throughout the end of classical antiquity.

The delicacy and reverence for what can only have originated from divine design was portrayed with such care, skill, and focused attention to detail and nuance. That classical feminine face, those fragile fingers and toes, the subtle creases and smooth, round surfaces—even when chiseled from solid stone. Amazing! And these works of art live on to inspire even generations of young artists today.

From an old engraving, I sketch out *Greek Goddess* with that very reverence in mind, and try to give special consideration to that highly recognized style of the ancients. To use a cliche' from the current art community, we all truly stand on the shoulders of giants.

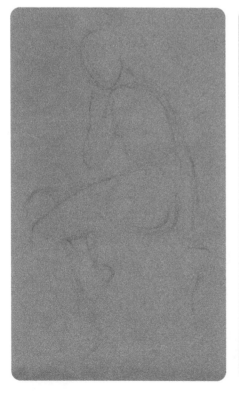

1

2

3

"Cowering Girl," 11 x 14 in., Graphite & Color Pencil on Toned Paper   47

SEATED POSES
Obstinate Beauty

Graphite & Color Pencil on Pastel Toned Paper
9 x 12 in.

For *Obstinate Beauty* as well as *Soft and Strong* (opposite), I thought I might play with color opposites between support and media, the yellow toned paper and the dark purple Prismacolor pencil (below), and the orange toned paper with indigo blue color pencil (opposite). It's often difficult to go wrong when playing off complimentary colors and opposites in regard to the color wheel. When in doubt, experiment with time-proven pairings.

Of course those color differences would mean very little without the value contrast between light and dark which really gives these two pieces their ultimate appeal and finality. Thus the white highlights (also achieved in color pencil).

Seated poses can sometimes feel static, commonplace and uninteresting, because in reality we—more often than not—see the figure in a seated position, so it can be fun to twist and turn the model into more thoughtful and uncommon angles to create a sense of attitude, thougtfulness or longing.

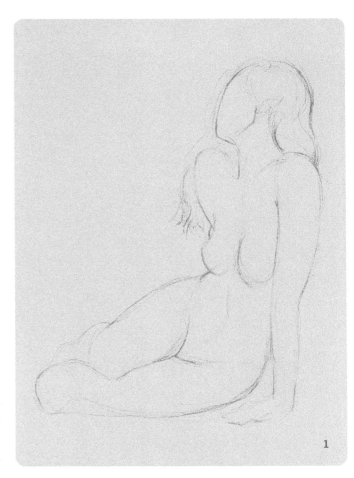

LIFE DRAWING STUDIES

SEATED POSES
GESTURES & 15–45 MINUTE SKETCHES

We know gesture drawing is a laying in of the action, form, and pose of a model/ figure. And that a few of its characteristics include: exploring form and feeling, drawing what you see as you see it, and using expressive marks. However, do these concise definitions not also apply to a more rendered sketch from life as seen here? Defined then, gesture drawing (the sketches near the bottom of the spread) must also include, quite simply, a *quick* sketch in which your hand follows your eyes *in a short amount of time*, often in as little as 30 seconds, or as long as 5 minutes. As in the section previous, the pieces toward the top and middle of the spread would not be counted as gestures, but still a grand excercise in improvement and progression.

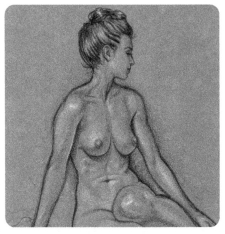

"Highlights and Curve," 12 x 16 in., Charcoal & Nupastel on Toned Paper

"Debbie Lounging," 14 x 11 in., Charcoal & Nupastel on Toned Paper

"Sun Hat," 14 x 11 in., Charcoal & Nupastel on Toned Paper

"Softer Thoughts," 12 x 16 in., Charcoal on Acrylic Paper

"Cami Relaxing," 16 x 12 in., Charcoal on Acrylic Paper

RECLINING POSES

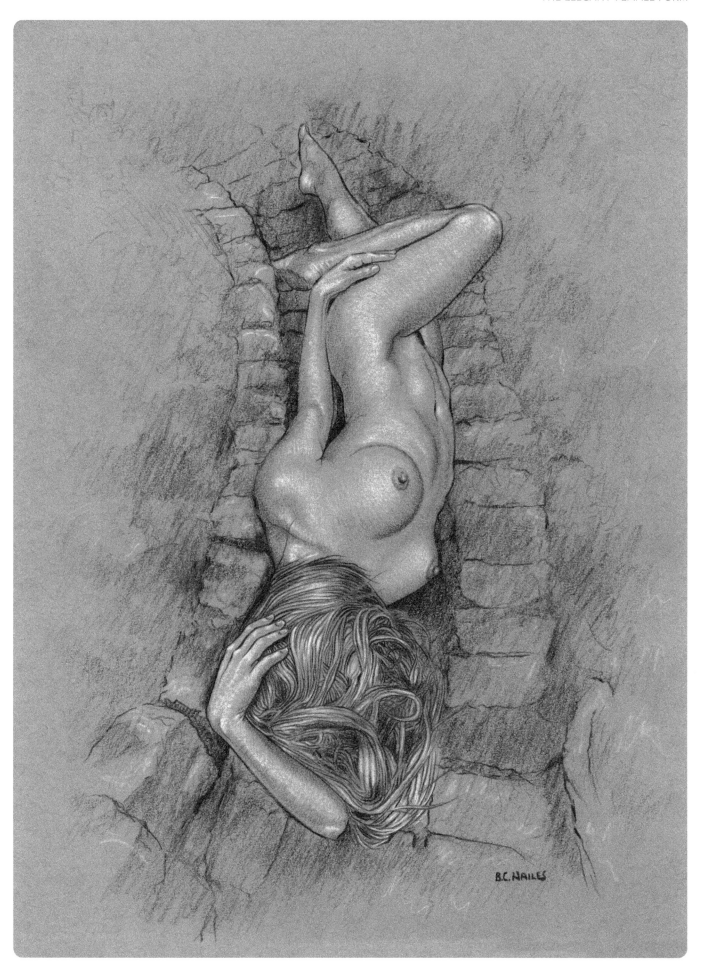

RECLINING POSES
CLASSICAL RECLINE

Graphite & Color Pencil on Toned Paper
14 x 11 in.

Every artist must become proficient at making decisions. The model, the pose, the lighting, the timing, and everything else that comprises a life drawing session are all challenges to be dealt with. But there are aspects you control, such as materials; pencil works great for light preliminary marks in the planning or development stages, charcoal allows you to cover large areas easily and make tonal adjustments as needed, whereas ink and paint make fairly indelible marks and can necessitate a certain overall size. Your position also has an effect on the outcome, so make sure you have a good and clear view of the model. Standing up can often give a better scope to look around the pose and to stand back from the easel to better gauge proportion. Be sure to take your time in looking at the model. Then look again. Many highly polished and refined life drawings can showcase dodgy proportions, so spend a little extra time analyzing the pose before you make your first marks on paper. Then lightly sketch out the basic shapes. Be fluid. Don't get too focused on drawing the outlines that you forget the body is a solid, three-dimensional form. Try drawing from the center outwards and apply tone from the outset or immediately after you have the basic, major forms worked out. Think of your subject rather than style. If you truly concentrate on observation, you can pretty much disregard 'style' and 'detail' altogether as those elements will come naturally. Pause. Step back and analyze your piece. Does it look right? is the entire figure in? Does the drawing rest comfortably on the support?

If it does, carry on. if not, then what should you change? Take your time building the composition. Don't rush into the details before you are happy with the composition and proportions. Lastly, get to know your model. Life drawing is a collaborative process, and the model is your creative partner. Chat with them. Get to know them. Involve them in the process. It can only lift the mood of the session.

RECLINING POSES
WISHING FOR HIGHER PURPOSE

Graphite, Color Pencil & Acrylic on Illustration Board
16 x 12 in.

In the listings for two of my previous figure drawing books, a few critics have suggested they are too advanced for beginners, while others have said they work great for all artists or skill levels.

My suggestion for beginners would be to focus on Step 1 of the many process drawings offered throughout these works. Just focus your practice on the basic proportions and layout of the figure, the basic shapes, and simple contours.

For students or intermediate artists, of course you will want to try your hand at more developed pieces, perhaps focusing solely on steps 1-2 or 1-3, repetition being the starting point for progression. And of course, add your own style and flavoring to the recipe.

For advanced artists, to get the most out of this book, take it merely as inspiration and either draw from your own models, perhaps using ideas for poses or style/media options offered herein. Or feel free to try your own hand at the model pics and/or drawings present to up your own artistic game.

1

2

3

1   2

3   4

RECLINING POSES
GRAVITY

Graphite & Color Pencil on Hahnemuhle Ingres Paper
9.4 x 12.2 in.

Some might consider the following six drawing steps as essential, but there are departures in some approaches:

1. Acquire a sure hand. *How* you hold pencil, charcoal, etc. is important, but nevertheless remains personal.

2. Choose your subject. Start with *simple* subjects, such as still lifes, before undertaking more complex compositions (landscapes, portraits). To compose your subject, follow your intuition!

3. Learn how to diagram. Your eye must do substantial analytical work. Once you have selected your subject, you need to study it from every angle. Practice representing the selected subject diagrammatically, by taking the forms and geometric volumes as your basis.

4. Take *sketching* **notes.** Draw snapshots of your subject from different angles, camera-style. For static subjects, work on rough sketches from various points of view to figure out volumes and changes in light. For moving subjects. such as human beings or animals, learn how to observe movements and postures.

5. Sketch with detail. Once you have all the information you need to start putting your drawing on paper, you can get your feet wet. Choose the angle of view, lighting, movement, etc. Sketch the first lines of your drawing with light strokes.

6. Do (many) studies. In your research lab for detail work, don't hold back, multiply your preliminary exercises on varied papers, boards and other supports. Test various values/gray tones, shade off, and use hatching. Discover for yourself the many possible drawing techniques!

1

2

3

4

"Meagan's World," 12 x 9 in., Color Pencil on Pastel Toned Paper

"Waking Up," 12.2 x 9.4 in., Color Pencil on Toned Paper

"Relax," 12.2 x 9.4 in., Color Pencil on Toned Paper

RECLINING POSES
ANGELS SLEEP

Graphite, Color Pencil & Acrylic on Canson Mixed Media
Artboard
16 x 12 in.

Sometimes the soft, quiet moments can deliver the heaviest impressions. In *Angels Sleep*, I wanted to convey a sense of restful longing and frame the central figure in an amalgam of comfortable and chaotic space amidst the folded and twisting sheets.

Lightly placed contour lines to start, followed quickly by oil-based color pencil in black to begin to eccentuate the shadows, which try to escape from the direct light source, and thereafter followed by thin, watered down glazes of neutral gray, raw umber, and black acrylic to almost give a gentle watercolor feel.

For the final stage, we'll continue to push the retreating shadow areas deeper, refine the softer edges, and add in a bit more color and chaos into the angel's surroundings with tiny splatters of grey purple, a warm 'fleshy' grey and lemon yellow. Sweet dreams or troubling nightmares can come unbidden. They might often grace or trouble our wakeful days and stretched out nights, but when angels sleep, which is it for them? I'll leave that to you to decide.

1

2

3

4

LIFE
STUDIES

"Innocence of Youth," 12.2 x 9.4 in., Graphite & Color Pencil on Toned Paper

RECLINING POSES

GESTURES & 15–30 MINUTE SKETCHES

Reclining poses often call for a horizontal or landscape picture plane, while standing poses generally require a vertical or portrait orientation. When you do enough of them, many sketches can start to feel the same or, at the very least, quite similar. When this happens, it tends to push us out of our regular way of thinking and working, almost forcing us to try a new approach. We might ask the models to switch it up. We might try a new paper or board material. We might start experimenting with media we're not accustomed to. We might try turning our horizontal paper vertical to focus on details or interesting areas of the figure that stand out to us. We may even attempt to alter our way of thinking and approach the figure as a landscape.

"The Water's Edge," 12.2 x 9.4 in., Charcoal on Toned Paper

"Beauty in the Breakdown," 12.2 x 9.4 in., Color Pencil on Toned Paper

"To Be Human," 12 x 9 in., Color Pencil on Pastel Toned Paper

"Recumbent," 12 x 9 in., Color Pencil on Toned Paper

KNEELING POSES

B.C. HAILES

KNEELING POSES

KNEELING TOWARD THE LIGHT

Graphite & Ink on Watercolor Board
12 x 16 in.

This stocato, cross-hatching ink style is something I experimented with in a few illustrations from one of my earlier works, *Passion & Spirit: The Dance Quote Book*. It's a fun way to loosen up and play impressionist with simple black fineliner micro-pens.

I still begin the drawing with light graphite outlines to map out the major forms (1 & 2), then with ink, I start to add detail and loose jumpy lines to accentuate the shadow areas (3) and major contours. Then, once we have our figure layed out in rather straightforward terms, the real fun begins (4). The key is using a careful mix of rhythm and chaos; random jerky lines used in tandem with directional lines that follow the form of objects brings together a nice balance amidst a nicely textured picture plane overall. It gives the impression of a black and white impressionistic painting, yet it's not a painting at all. Merely a simple ink drawing. This style is definitely worth trying out, if only for the fun of experimentation.

1

2

3

KNEELING POSES
ARCHERESS ON WHITE

Graphite, Color Pencil & Acrylic on Watercolor Board
12 x 16 in.

The iconic and dramatic pose of the archeress, both powerul and inspiring, sans the arrow—perhaps a symbol of burying one's weapons of war in lieu of a peaceful and loving life.

Begin with light gesture lines to reveal the basic form (1). Flesh out the contours, still with a soft application in graphite (2). Once the basic figure is worked out, refinement and detail is introduced, using primarily chiaroscuro, the juxtaposition of darks and lights as well as texture to find the right form in each part and plane of the figure (3). With light source and cast shadow placement foremost in mind, white, black and gray acrylic paint is brought in to punch up the texture, value play and overall finished quality of the piece (4). As classical figures that we've seen extensively throughout Medieval, Roman and Greek cultures as well as in times more ancient, the form of the archer and archeress have not lost their appeal, whether in the realm of fine art or even pop culture today. There is just something about a man or woman drawing back that taut bowstring.

1

2

3

4

SELKIE OF THE SEA

Graphite, Color Pencil & Acrylic on Illustration Board
15 x 20 in.

Backlit figures can be an interesting challenge to tackle. For this ethereal piece entitled, *Selkie of the Sea*, I wanted to convey a kind of natural magic that happens on the sunlit waves at dusk, almost silhouetting the semi-realistic figure against an impressionistic backdrop.

A Celtic and Norse mythology-inspired theme of the mythical sea folk that can change their form from seal to human simply by shedding their skin, it lends itself to the romantic, much like the folktales of mermaids, nymphs and fairies. The legend of the selkies originates from the Northern Isles of Scotland, and is rich with fanciful concepts just waiting to be explored.

My initial lines (1) quickly complicated themselves in detail—probably to a fault (2-3), and then with acrylic, I felt the urge to pull back that detail and paint out much of it by way of brushstroke, simplifying the overall feel of the piece using color and contrast here and there, or a lack thereof (4).

1

4

KNEELING POSES
TOUCH OF A ROSE

Graphite, Color Pencil & Acrylic on Watercolor Board
12 x 16 in.

it may seem obvious to some painters that the illusion created by chiaroscuro is vastly superior to that created by any type of 'contour method'. However, if that is truly the case, is the 'contour method' as seen across this spread (and many others throughout this book) wholly without merit? And if so, why did so many of us ever start using it?

It seems to me that actually it's not without merit in the sense that if we took a human finger for example, there are actually natural lines on it, which fold around the cylindrical surface of the finger. The same is true with facial features that will change in shape, size and distribution according to the expressions of the face. In fact even roses or apples sometimes possess these lines. So in some sense part of what conveys that these objects are three-dimensional is how surface features curve around the body of the object.

To paint a smooth billiard ball without such features, a classical chiaroscuro approach does tend to make more practical sense, as used in the final steps here (3-4).

1

2

3

4

KNEELING POSES
LE PETIT ANGE

Graphite & Color Pencil on Toned Paper
9.4 x 12.2 in.

The Little Angel kneels on the edge between shadow and light (4). Understanding these *value* differences is almost synonymous with understanding *light* and *form*. One can't really exist without the other two. The combination of light and shadow creates a range of values, which then creates the illusion of form. Because depicting value and form depends so much on light, one needs to understand how light behaves when it illuminates a form. Luckily, when light falls on different forms, it acts in predictable ways. So you can study how light falls on such basic forms as spheres, cylinders, cones, etc., which are variably prevalent in most figurative pieces. When we render the figure or portrait, we almost subconsciously combine these basic three-dimensional shapes to create the intricate, complex forms of the body. Bullet points? Elements of form in the *light* family include: 1. Direct light 2. Highlight 3. Half-tone. Elements of form in the *shadow* family: 1. Core shadow 2. Reflected light 3. Cast shadow 4. Occlusion shadow.

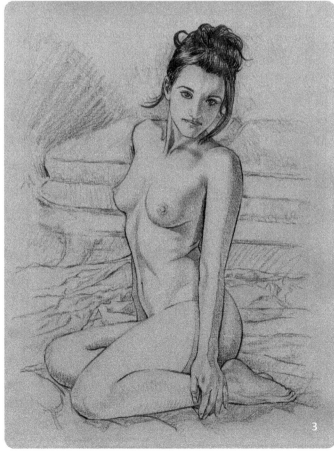

KNEELING POSES

THE LITTLE MERMAID

Graphite & Color Pencil on Toned Pastel Paper
9 x 12 in.

A classic theme. A beloved fairytale A powerful pose. With this quick color pencil sketch, I wanted to show that a concept doesn't need to be complicated to find its 'happily ever after.'

Beginning the process with simple sketch work in graphite (1 & 2), I break into color with Tuscan red for the hair and indigo blue for everything else (3). Dropping in deeper values by using higher pressure with the indigo for shadows and white and cream for highlights, I finish it off with tones of orange, burnt ochre, peach, black raspberry, lilac, and canary yellow (4).

For an artist who dreams of life experience and becoming part of something more, a good place to start is doing sketches like these—a whole lot of them. With every drawing and every painting, you'll get that much closer to realizing your ultimate goals. Practice might not make your artworks perfect, but if you create a certain many, you're virtually guaranteed to find your legs in no time.

LIFE DRAWING STUDIES

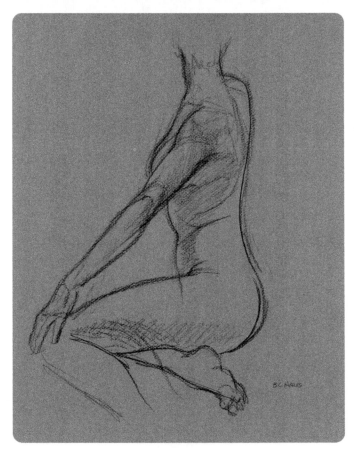

BENDING POSES

BENDING POSES
PEERING OVER THE EDGE

Graphite & Color Pencil on Toned Paper
11 x 14 in.

I don't always think about academic lists or procedures as I work, but it can sometimes be helpful for beginners to commit certain of these teachngs to memory and draw upon them every so often (no pun intended). So let's reflect briefly on the 6 principles of design: 1. *Balance* in design is similar to balance in physics. It provides stability and structure. It's the weight distributed in the design by the placement of your elements. 2. *Proximity* creates relationship between elements. It provides a focal point. Proximity doesn't mean that elements have to be placed together, it means they should be visually connected in some way. 3. *Alignment* allows us to create order and organisation. Aligning elements allows them to create a visual connection with each other. 4. *Repetition* strengthens a design by tying together individual elements. It helps to create association and consistency. Repetition can create rhythm (a feeling of organized movement). 5. *Contrast* is the juxtaposition of opposing elements. It allows us to emphasize or highlight key elements in your design. 6. *Space* refers to the distance or area between, around, above, below, or within elements. Both positive and negative space are important factors to be considered in every design.

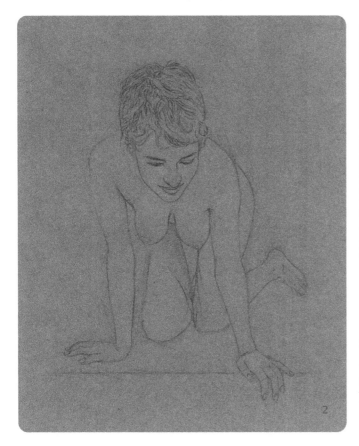

BENDING POSES
READY DANCER

Graphite, Color Pencil & Acrylic on Canson Illustration Board
12 x 16 in.

True dancers are disciplined. They know their bodies well. They understand how to push themselves. And they are accustomed to affecting others, even *moving* them by way of their own movement, form, and line. Like such dancers, I believe artists ought to employ these same qualities to their own work ethic. We may not all be able to flit across a stage or command an audience with our strength and grace, but like a dance performed at a ballet or classical theatre, we can imbue our works with a similar kind of magic: the magic to make others *feel*.

We might start off the show with soft, flitting marks (1), followed by more deliberate strokes (2), adding meaning and form to the story or struggle of which we're telling, each step of the way. After all, every piece is a story of light versus darkness, and all the values in between (3). And then, at the grand finale, we may try to wow our patrons with bold and sporadic splashes of color and texture to give a certain finality and closure to the piece (4).

1

2

3

BENDING POSES
SWASHBUCKLER

Graphite, Color Pencil & Acrylic on Watercolor Board
12 x 16 in.

Coming up with creative and dynamic poses can be accomplished in multiple ways, including (but not limited to) experimentation with reference models, comic art samples, screen shots from film or television, online photo scrap and other media, or even your ever active imagination alone.

To draw or enhance incredible action poses, a focus on anatomy can be key for realistic and dynamic drawings, enabling you to understand muscle coordination, proportion and relative shapes. With adequate knowledge of anatomy, you can add life to your characters. Moreover, understanding the movements of the body can also help you to draw without references. However, don't feel bad about using reference. All beginners do it, and even the greatest art masters use models and photo scrap regularly.

Having an in-depth or comprehensive knowledge of underlying anatomy is ideal, and can take more than a lifetime to obtain, but it's not necessary to start drawing the action figure. Just recognizing basic clusters of muscles or understanding anatomical dimensionality or even simple shapes and relationships when muscles are flexed (and expand) or relaxed (and contract) can be enough. To attain this basic (and cumulative) level of knowledge, the answer is simple: observe what you see around you . . . and then add a little spice to it.

1

2

3

4

BENDING POSES
LADY OF STRUGGLE

Graphite & Color Pencil on Hahnemuhle Ingres Toned
Paper
12.2 x 9.4 in.

Seated or bending poses can sometimes look stale, so you can exaggerate the curves and proportions from what you might see in your models to breathe more life into the drawing. However, if you push it too far, you'll approach the caricature arena, so look for that balance.

Also, if you happen to think drawing an athletic or muscular human figure is a struggle, try a horse. You'll be back to human figures in no time.

As demonstrated before, I like to begin the drawing with soft, thin line work, then, once the major forms are established, I move to a bolder gesture line to accentuate the curves of the figures, adding a bit more detail with each pass. Once the contours are satisfying, I'll go in and add some tonal shadows in color pencil which you'll see in the final renderings (3-4).

With fully-rendered drawings, the temptation is to either quit too early or over-render your piece, and so it becomes difficult to know exactly when to stop and call your artwork finished. For those of you who believe in the Holy Ghost, rely on whisperings of the Spirit. For those of you who don't, you'll just have to use your best judgement. Or you can ask around. Your family will most likely have something to say, and the peanut gallery will always be full of opinions on just about any matter. Joking aside, when the piece *feels* complete or comes to a stage when the marks you are making are not adding anything to its overall quality, or even worse, lessening the piece, you should know to simply walk away.

The struggle is real.

1

2

3

4

BENDING POSES
FLEXIBILITY

Graphite & Color Pencil on Toned Paper
9.4 x 12.2 in.

For any real figure artist to say they enjoy drawing dancers is likely an understatement. To borrow a few adjectives from the listing of one of my other illustrated works entitled *Passion & Spirit: The Dance Quote Book*, strength, vulnerability, grace, and beauty don't even scratch the surface of communicating the essence of a true dancer.

Why are they so fun to draw? Well, hopefully the adjoining examples show what can't adequately be told by means of words on the page. Like artists know their pencils and brushes, a dancer knows her body. That knowledge translates through how they perform, hold a pose, or even hold their body when they're not posing. The movement, the angles, the endless possibilities, all wrapped up in a virtuoso of visual rhythm. To try and capture that magic is a real treat, and a feat in and of itself. A feat that requires practice. Lots and lots of practice, but then, anything worth doing is worth doing well, and like dancers spending dozens of hours for weeks at a time preparing for that big performance, we must put in the effort, for beauty (and talent) must be shared.

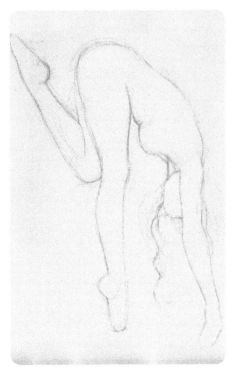

1

2

3

BENDING POSES
THE GOLDEN SHOE

Graphite & Color Pencil on Hahnemuhle Ingres Toned
Paper
9.4 x 12.2 in.

Created for the back cover of *Draw It With Me: A Study of the Human Form*, I wanted *The Golden Shoe* to portray a sense of distance and simultaneous sensual connection between the couple shown. As if they've just had an argument, but are simultaneously preparing for a calendared date night. That push-and-pull of real-world relationships causes a sort of tension, and to carry it further, a *story*.

Trained as an illustrator as well as designer on the collegiate level, I've always loved and been drawn to the idea of story. Stories are what make life interesting. They must contain character(s), setting, conflict and plot to be considered a story. Often, a single illustration may contain all four of these elements.

So is it crucial for every piece of art to contain the four elements of story or at least hint at them? Of course not. But it's certainly fun when they do.

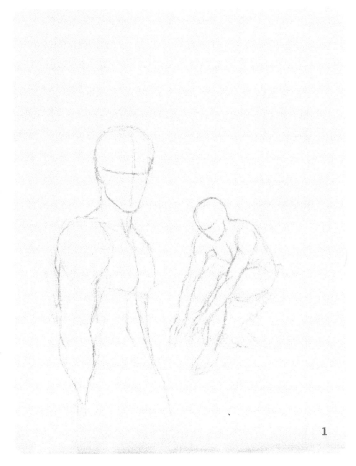

1

2

3

4

LIFE DRAWING STUDIES

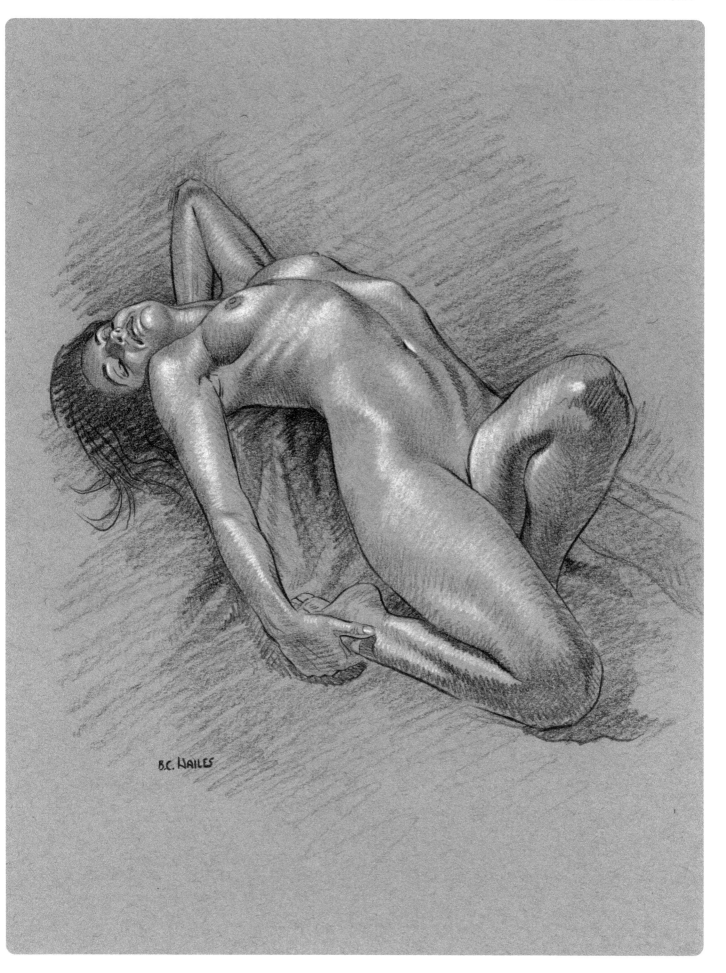

BENDING POSES
GESTURES & 30–45 MINUTE SKETCHES

Bending poses can obviously be interpreted in a lot of different ways, practically as many ways as the body can lean, bend, double over or sway. There's actually no limit to the types of poses that can be exhibited or portrayed. That's part of what makes figure drawing so exciting. There's always a new, fresh pose or angle to capture in your own unique style. Whether sketching out what you see in quick gesture (bottom right), or spending a little more time in a life drawing session to try and emulate the general feel of the model's pose, it's always a welcome challenge. And one that forces the artist to dig deep and really try to answer the question that deep thinkers have pondered for millennia: what is it that makes us human?

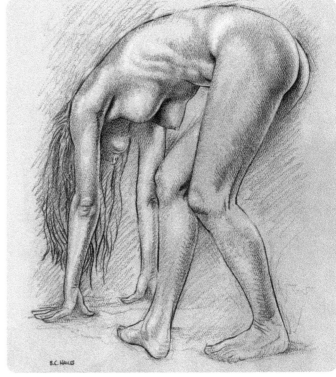

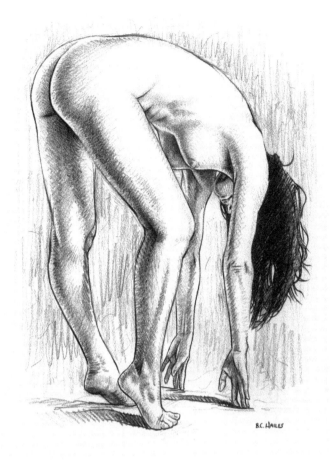

CROUCHING POSES

"Girl Crouching in an Evening Gown," 11 x 14 in., Color Pencil & Nupastel on Toned Paper   111

CROUCHING POSES
CURLED

Graphite on Illustration Board
12 x 16 in.

I find sometimes as I plan and construct a drawing, I approach the action in a similar manner to the way a builder might approach a given architectural development, line upon line, simple to complicated, foundations before details. Consider for a moment the step-by-step process to build a house:

1. *Prepare Construction Site & Pour Foundation*
2. *Complete Rough Framing*
3. *Complete Rough Plumbing, Electrical and HVAC*
4. *Install Insulation*
5. *Complete Drywall & Interior Fixtures; Start Exterior Finishes*
6. *Finish Interior Trim; Install Exterior Walkways & Driveway*
7. *Install Hard Surface Flooring and Countertops; Complete Exterior Grading*
8. *Finish Mechanical Trims; Install Bathroom Fixtures*
9. *Install Mirrors and Shower Doors; Finish Flooring & Exterior Landscaping*
10. *Conduct Final Walk-Through.*

1

2

3

B.C. NAILES

4

CROUCHING POSES
SURRENDER

Graphite, Color Pencil & Nupastel on Toned Paper
12 x 16 in.

The foundations of a drawing, including composition (i.e. format management, framing, full & empty spaces, etc.), proportions (i.e. the ratios of the various parts to each other and of details to the whole), and balance (i.e. the alignment of various reference points along a vertical axis, such as the head with respect to the feet in the example shown here), should always be put into service, but also investing your own personal experience, your world vision, and, of course, your own artistic sensibilites.

For *"Surrender,"* I wanted to offer a soft, illustrative quality in regard to the centrally-placed figure that suggests a silent yet commanding respect, all tethered in the contemplative beauty of the face. To help accomplish this, I placed most value contrast there, and let the rest loosen up and die off to abstraction for her surroundings. To make the point of her decided submission, they matter not. Thus, the fully and carefully rendered facial features, head and neck, and the loosely scribbled wilderness to the ouskirts around her.

CROUCHING POSES
ON THE PROWL

Graphite & Color Pencil on Toned Paper
12.2 x 9.4 in.

One of the great features of drawing dynamic action poses is the lack of perfectly vertical or horizontal lines found in and around the human form, which tends to heighten the action, tension, or uneasiness of the piece overall. Like the fluidity of the dancer in flight or a prowling animal in natural movement through its surroundings.

Also, the way light reacts to and wraps around the softly changing planes of the body brings with it a supple, inviting quality in the shading of the skin. To enphasize that soft beauty of the curvature of light resting flatteringly on the figure, I take more care in the areas of the face, neck and chest, amping up the high value contrast between darkest darks and lightest lights in and around those regions, allowing myself to let go as I move out and away from those focal points until arriving at the imaginary background, where it becomes an almost scribbled cartoon style of sketching, nearly a doodle one might find on a napkin at a restaurant or on the outer margins of a dreaded math assignment.

1

2

3

4

CROUCHING POSES
SEARCHING FOR REFLECTION

Graphite, Color Pencil & Acrylic on Illustration Board
12 x 16 in.

For *Searching for Reflection*, I wanted to portray a quiet moment. Something raw and natural, contemplative and organic with the figure. As though one had stumbled upon a mythological scene in the woods to behold some sort of fairy, siren, or hallucinated beauty at the water's edge, unaware or unacknowledging of any viewer. Thus, the limited palette of phthalocyanine green, raw umber, and Payne's grey. The first two colors were applied to the background with reckless abandon, and the grey reserved for in and around her figure (4).

The delicate pose with one arm reaching down toward the water's surface, and the falling hair are worked out basically in the first stage (1), and carefully developed with added detail (2-3), keeping the contours of shaded areas with heavier lines and curves or highlighted areas generally lighter and thinner. The soft shading around the flesh helps the figure to stand out against the more rough and tumble made-up backdrop. But the darkness of the hair really makes it pop.

1

2

3

CROUCHING POSES
HUMAN WEAPON

Graphite, Color Pencil & Posca Marker on Toned Paper
11 x 14 in.

I happen to love *Bond, Bourne,* and the *Dark Knight* as well as the next man, but since writing and illustrating the spy thriller, *Blink,* I'm all in for the genre.

The photo to the right was taken among some of my unused reference material for *Blink, the Illustrated Novel,* but I have a hard time letting good reference go to waste, so embellished futuristic body armor or not, I had to make use of it. Whether this is considered a kneeling pose, a crouching pose, or both, I thought I'd like to include it in this volume so as to illustrate the variety one might find while attempting to capture the elegant female form.

Even below the handguns, the authentic police carry belt, and the certified Chinese diving suit, the beautiful and dangerous figure still shows through just fine, and must be respected. Especially considering the confident, deadly, and unpredictable attitude of the shot. Step aside, Ethan Hunt, and make way for this new breed of *Human Weapon.*

CROUCHING POSES
HEADS AND TAILS

Graphite on Bristol Board
14 x 11 in.

As artists, some days we feel inspired, full of ideas, and ready to tackle the abstract or concrete concepts floating around inside our heads. And at other times, it's all we can do to simply try to draw what's in front of us.

Life is ups, downs, and holding patterns. And so it is with the production of art. The key is *consistent* production.

If a student is given an assignment to create one and only one perfect masterpiece over the span of a semester, and another student is told they must produce three original artworks every week during that same semester, who will truly produce the masterpiece? The student assigned *quality* or *quantity*? The answer will always be the student producing *quantity*. Because the quality comes with practice. And among the many pieces produced by the *quantity* student, several are sure to stand out, what from happy accidents, thoroughly honed skills acquired through the rigorous deadlines, and that oh so blossoming talent. When it comes down to it, I believe talent is merely a desire to do something a lot. It's taking pleasure in that practice one feels drawn to (no pun intended). It's true we all wish for a higher purpose, but until we arrive there, there is always time to create something beautiful.

1

2

3

LIFE DRAWING STUDIES

CROUCHING POSES

GESTURES & 30–45 MINUTE SKETCHES

When choosing a pose for a figure drawing, not every pose the model strikes will be right, and not every photo reference is going to be perfect. Look for poses that are natural and balanced, not stiff or boring. Some movement or tension can make the pose more interesting, but even in a crouch, your subject should look stable and comfortable in the position. The mix of creativity between model and artist is one of the elements that has made figure drawing from life a staple of any serious figurative artist over time. Drawing the human figure in a plethora of poses under different lighting from various angles and in front of varying backgrounds will always keep the practice fresh and exciting. And while practice doesn't necessarily make perfect, it makes for definite improvement.

THE FIGURE
IN MOTION

"The Lively Goddess," 12 x 16 in., Graphite, Color Pencil & Acrylic on Illustration Board   129

THE FIGURE IN MOTION
DANCE FREE

Graphite & Color Pencil on Toned Pastel Paper
9 x 12 in.

Working on toned paper—whatever the color—is always nice because it takes care of a range of midtones before you even begin. It allows you to focus solely on the shadows and highlights of the lit model or reference photograph you are working from. You can make decisions along the way based solely on where the darkest darks and the lightest lights should fall, not having to shade or color in much by way of mid-range values.

On most of the toned paper pieces throughout this book, I've laid in the darks first, then changed my focus to the white highlights to finish them off. For this piece, entitled *Dance Free,* I thought I'd switch it up in keeping with the feel and theme of the pose. If we get too stale or set in our ways, our work can suffer. Sometimes it can be quite freeing to let loose and shake up our approach to an artwork, even if we are using familiar media and supports we're comfortable with. Leaving one's comfort zone is key to growth and progression, both in life and in art.

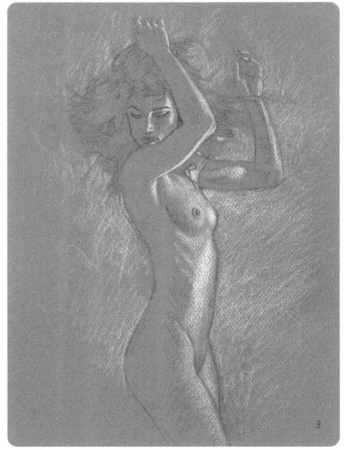

B.C. HAILES

4

THE FIGURE IN MOTION
FISH IN THE SEA

Graphite, Color Pencil & Acrylic on Illustration Board
15 x 20 in.

B.C. HAILES

THE FIGURE IN MOTION
TO THE RESCUE

Graphite, Color Pencil & Acrylic on Bristol Board
11 x 14 in.

Back to a feeling from some of my earlier comic book/ graphic novel roots, this was a lively pose to illustrate. From a photoshoot with one of my go-to models, Lea, I knew going into it that the foreshortening would be a challenge, especially working off a photograph after the fact (because we all know photos can lie), but it proved an exacting problem to solve.

As per usual, I began with soft, thin line work in graphite, then quickly moved on to my preferrred oil-based Color Pencil pencils (dark purple) once I had the major forms established as a guide to proportion. Then came the details (often, the most enjoyable part). Varying line width and subtle shading strokes applied with flitting motion helped to support and retain the implied movement of the piece. Otherwise, such a pose can become static and . . . well . . . *posed*. Finished off with some more precisely focused shading in areas of interest and haphazard brush strokes (in bone black acrylic & much water) with fairly erratic flicks of the wrist, again, for movement's sake.

1

2

3

B.C. NAILES

4

THE FIGURE IN MOTION
VIRTUOSO

Graphite & Color Pencil on Toned Paper
11 x 14 in.

When composing a piece containing a single, centrally placed figure, it can sometimes make the composition more interesting to add even simple background elements, such as lines, textures, obscure clouds of darks and lights, or any number of things, thus dividing the empty space and making the picture plane more interesting to look at overall.

However, one must be careful about avoiding *tangents*. Tangents are where two lines just touch each other in a way that causes spatial ambiguity and a slight jarring on our eyes. It's not super obvious but can really ruin a perfectly good drawing or painting, and can unwittingly change the composition in your artwork. You'll notice in *Virtuoso* that the girl's hands, feet, and torso don't quite touch the vertical lines spanning the page from top to bottom, nor do they overlap (which would also be fine). There is just enough space between her hand and that vertical dividing line to tease without adding discomfort for the viewer. If her fingers barely touched that line, that would be a tangent, and that would be a no-no.

1

2

3

4

THE FIGURE IN MOTION
SILVER & GOLD

Graphite & Acrylic on Illustration Board
12 x 16 in.

Sometimes it can be fun to experiment with taking a reference photo and changing the premise altogether. For instance, rather than having the girl resting her back leg on the table or radio shelf, we could have her flying through a skyward stream of silver and gold. We can change the polka dot bikini to the same golden color as the background, so her silver (graphite) skin will stand out all the more, giving the focus to the girl's nice pose and action lines.

Occasionally, one can overwork a piece or find that it doesn't come out quite the way you imagine to begin with. That's quite all right, and it happens to all artists. A lot, as it turns out. It happened to me with this particular work. I actually prefer the step 2 version shown below over the finish in 3, perhaps due to the extra contrast of the bright white figure against the darker background, or maybe because the silver streams didn't quite add to the piece like I thought they would. Others might prefer the final, but that just means art is subjective, and that will always be the case.

1

2

3

"Water Nymph" 12 x 16 in. Graphite, Color Pencil & Acrylic on Watercolor Board

"Study of Undine Rising From the Waters," 9 x 12 in., Color Pencil on Toned Paper

LIFE DRAWING STUDIES

THE FIGURE IN MOTION
60 MINUTE MIXED MEDIA SKETCHES

Obviously, it can be difficult to draw the human figure from life when that figure is jumping, flying or twisting in mid-air or swimming, flipping or diving underwater. Even dynamic action poses that a model can't hold for more than a few seconds at a time would fall in this category of problematic sketching scenarios. Thus, we are reserved to working from photographs or other types of reference to work from. For the pieces shown here, I wanted to play around with mixed media, utilizing the strengths of ink, graphite and acrylic all together in a selection of aggressive and compelling poses of the female form in about as lively positions as anyone could manage. Girls of taut action can be a joy to draw.

"Splayed Out Front Crouch," 12 x 9 in., Graphite & Ink on Pastel Paper

"Valkyrie," 16 x 12 in., Graphite, Ink & Acrylic on Illustration Board

"Caustics," 12 x 16 in., Graphite, Ink & Acrylic on Illustration Board

THE PREGNANT FIGURE

B.C. HAILES

THE PREGNANT FIGURE

THE ANGEL INSIDE

Graphite, Color Pencil & Acrylic on Illustration Board
16 x 12 in.

Beginning with the ghost of a drawing in the opening stages allows for mistakes that when fixed later on, either don't even show up or acquire a look of intentionality; just added texture and hints of artifact left behind by the artist.

Even when using a monochromatic color scheme like this piece, *The Angel Inside*, in indigo, I still tend to use more than one color. You have the light hints of charcoal gray from the graphite (1-2), indigo blue Prismacolor pencil (3), and finally two colors in acrylic: Payne's grey (primarily on the figure), and Prussian blue.

The acrylics are used here only with subtle application, almost like a watercolor wash. I only prefer acrylic over watercolor because it holds its opaqueness and saturation much longer over time without fading, keeping the piece vibrant and alive. Also, it helps you to keep more control during the application process without causing nearly the flowering and meandering effects watercolor is famous for. Mixed with much water, I apply the paint in various tiny 'glazes', sometimes painting with water alone (especially around the outer edges of the figure), which subtely picks up traces of the graphite and color pencil to soften up even some of the underdrawing and sketch marks themselves. Overall, this gives the piece a more worked over and painterly appeal despite it being a rather 'simple' drawing.

1

2

3

B.C. HAILES

4

THE PREGNANT FIGURE
CHRISTIE WITH CHILD

Graphite, Color Pencil & Acrylic on Illustration Board
12 x 16 in.

There's nothing quite so glowing as a pregnant woman who loves her child, particularly when you happen to be married to her. I wanted to capture that glow in Christie's warm smile, so you'll notice the face is the focal point containing most of the detail and subtle care in rendering. As your eye moves away from the face, the detail levels and accuracy with which the pencil and paintbrush are applied diminishes.

I think most pieces are served best with one or two such focal points and a general 'loosening up' toward the outskirts. This is a hard concept to teach, and even to practice, for some more than others. Even after all these years and thousands of drawings, I still find myself imbuing too much detail in too much of the picture plane's real estate.

Still, we work. And we learn. And we improve. Little by little. Line by line. Shape by shape. Splotch of color by splotch of color. And by these small and simple things are great things brought to pass . . . And the journey takes much longer than ten months.

1

2

B.C. HAILES

THE PREGNANT FIGURE
QUEEN AND PRINCESS

Graphite, Color Pencil & Posca Marker on Toned Pastel Paper
9 x 12 in.

Backlit figures can be a nice challenge in terms of shading and finding value subtleties around the changing planes and curves, soft as they may appear. Making choices upfront about where the darkest darks and lightest lights will fall can make or break the final outcome, but if your reference material is of high enough quality, those levels and how the light attaches to your subject will be much easier to determine. Where the light glistens off of or shines out from behind the model (4), and the way you render it says a lot about your own personal style, and can open up for the artist a playground where any rules rather go out the window. That juxtaposition of careful and refined rendering for an accurate portrayal of form and proportions with a haphazard free-for-all of sketchy, scribbly outer marks can create an interesting look; a bit of sanity and insanity inhabiting the same space, perhaps not unlike the mind and thoughts of many artists. Most of the time, we keep our stuff together, appreciating the law and order of the world around us, and at the same time, every so often, we humans like to let loose. Even queens and princesses.

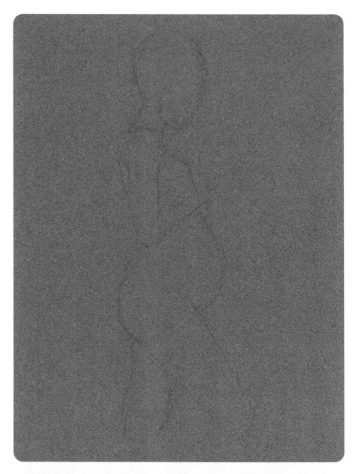

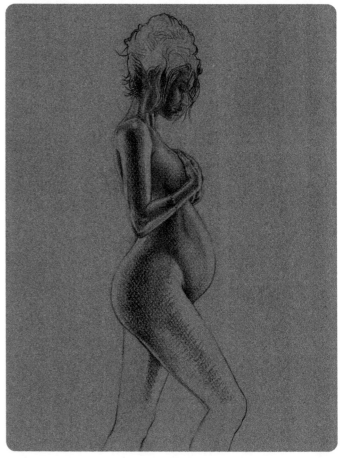

THE PREGNANT FIGURE
EXPECTING

Graphite, Color Pencil & Acrylic on Wood Panel
16 x 20 in.

With another piece completed for my *Maidens & Monsters* series, I wanted *Expecting* to be more about creating a mood than an actual narrative. So, the story behind the expectant young woman, the dingy marsh setting, the period dress, and the creepy, mysterious figure standing behind the girl with those glowing beady eyes, I leave open for the viewer's own personal interpretation.

As for the final rendering (4), I limited my palette of open acrylics to: Cadmium Red Dark, Yellow Ochre, Pthalo Blue, Raw Umber, Bone Black, and Zinc White. Using basically the primary colors, this forces one to mix all the subtleties of skin tones and natural undershades of the dismal background from scratch and by hand, Raw Umber being the exception. For the underpainting glaze, I mixed up some green tones with the Pthalo Blue and Yellow Ochre to amp up that dreary, organic look that would make that red gown and ornate crown really stand out, again reserving the focused detail and highest contrast for the girl's gaze.

1

THE PREGNANT FIGURE
WIFE AND MOTHER

Graphite on Illustration Board
16 x 20 in.

Having watched my own exquisite wife endure the physical and emotional struggle of five pregnancies (thus far), I can certainly appreciate the love and sacrifice that bringing a brand new pure and innocent spirit into the world entails. I know for most (if not all) women, it's no walk in the park, and to allow one's own body to be analyzed, poked, prodded, stretched, cut, sewn, used and abused, I believe there's a special place in Heaven reserved for these angelic ladies who are willing to give up so much on behalf of another.

So let's discuss the benefits of drawing them: One of the elements that makes figure drawing such a joy on its own is attempting to not only understand but execute well all the curves, mountains, valleys, angles, contours and depressions present in each unique human form. With pregant women, these elements are often magnified. Pregnant women also carry a special aura about them. And that divine calling of motherhood can bring with it a certain feeling to elevate any artwork to something truly thoughtful and meaningful.

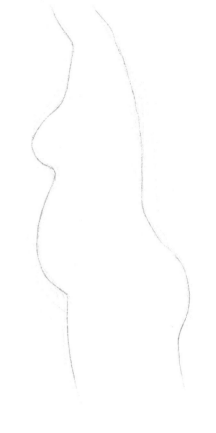

1

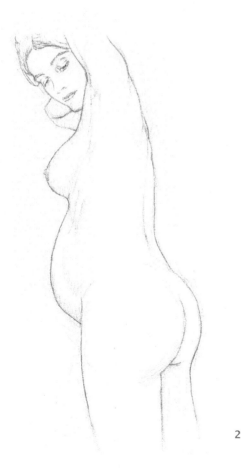

2

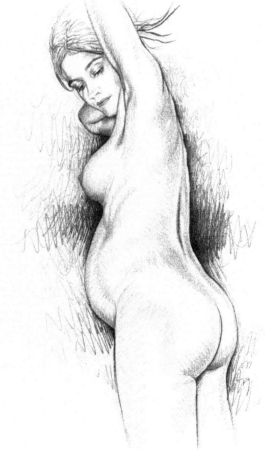

3

B.C. NAILES

4

THE PREGNANT FIGURE
JUST BREATHE

Graphite & Color Pencil on Toned Pastel Paper
12 x 9 in.

Once you establish a light sketch of the major proportions in contour (1-2), it can be an educational exercise to focus on the negative shapes of white space surrounding the figure (3) before dropping in the finishing shadows and details usually applied first (4).

Having attended my fair share of life drawing classes, I've noticed most students generally approach this practice of life drawing using only one or two different mediums (usually charcoal or graphite) on large newsprint or artist's paper pads as taught widely in artistic academia. There is certainly nothing wrong with these media or supports, but having learned so much myself switching things up and experimenting with a variety of not only media and supports, but also color, my horizons have been widened greatly, my mind opened, and my imagination more free to explore more ambiguous possibilities.

The more one practices, the more one comes to appreciate the importance of subtleties to their approach, such as not only line weight, but where you place the heavier shades versus lighter ones. With time and observation one comes to appreciate the masters' grasp of such things and the difficulty of application. However, (even though we do) we shouldn't compare ourselves to the masters, only master our own work and build upon it day by day, figure by figure, and scribble by scribble. And then, hopefully, one day we'll look back with pride in the progression we've made.

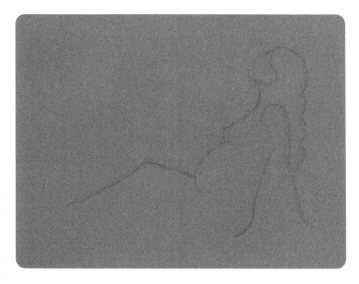

1

2

3

4

LIFE DRAWING STUDIES

THE PREGNANT FIGURE
30-60 MINUTE SKETCHES

While the growth and stages of pregnancy in a woman's body are nothing short of miraculous, it does seem to carry with it a certain weight of responsibility in portraying that beauty in form. I believe motherhood is something approaching the sacred, and should be treated with much care. For *Development* (top right), I wanted to show the steady advancement and expansion of the female form as well as the maturing that takes place when undergoing the feat of pregnancy, and so I attempt to represent that with a progression in technique from almost gesture to finely rendered pencil, as well as several steps in between. For *Womb (bottom right)*, I have encased the mother's figure in a womb-like space, and *Against a Wall* (below) speaks to the woman as strong, sensual and nurturing all at once.

"Against a Wall," 11 x 14 in., Charcoal & Nupastel on Toned Paper

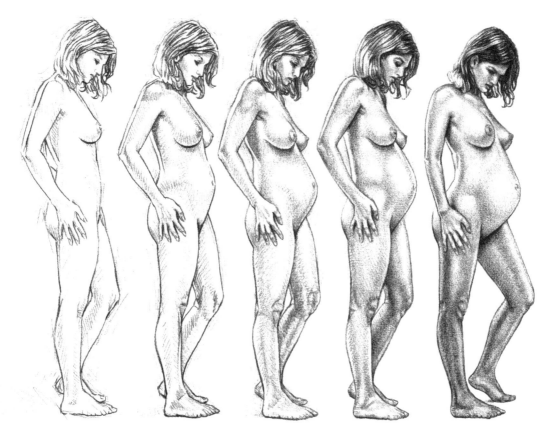

"Development," 16 x 12 in., Graphite on Illustration Board

"Womb," 12 x 9 in., Ink on Bristol Board

UNUSUAL POSES

UNUSUAL POSES
ON THE DUNES

Graphite, Color Pencil & Posca Marker on Toned Paper
12 x 9 in.

Anyone that attends life drawing classes regularly will inevitably encounter more challenging poses that appear *foreshortened*. For those unfamiliar with the term, foreshortening refers to the distortion that happens when we draw the human figure in space from an exaggerated or extreme point of view. It is simply what happens when the human form is viewed in perspective.

This is a wonderful exercise in seeing the figure more as a conglomeration of abstract shapes and relationships between masses rather than merely a human subject. And I often find the greatest challenge in regard to the foreshortened figure to be rendering the head and face correctly, as it tends to throw all basic conventions out the window. (So, whichever part(s) you happen to struggle with the most, practice it/them the most.)

The figure can be placed in an indefinite number of positions and in order to capture the figure in these specific types of poses, one must be able to recognize and replicate the distortion that exists in a pose. With the figure's basic proportions defined on the surface in light graphite (1-2), you can "thicken" things up by sketching the contour lines of the figure with confidence (3). Further refining, adding details and features, and emphasizing highlights and shadows can then be applied (4). The illusion of a light source, subtle or bold, can be attained through the addition of a range of value in chiaroscuro. Here, it was done using the color, Black Raspberry.

When the figure is in perspective as shown in these process sketches of *On the Dunes*, and foreshortening is a factor, if we can understand what we are seeing and how to create the required illusion on the drawing surface, we can be successful. It's all about distortion. The more extreme the angle and point of view, the greater the distortion. If we understand this and apply it to our figure drawings, then foreshortening is something that anyone can master.

1

2

3

4

UNUSUAL POSES
FOUNDATIONAL

Graphite, Color Pencil & Acrylic on Illustration Board
12 x 16 in.

Let's talk about gravity's effect on the human form. We are not plastic action figures, but we are also not amorphous blobs of jello or puddy. We're actually something in-between. Our underlying skeletal structures are a rigid framework with joints that only move in certain directions, upon which muscles, fat and skin build, stretch, and hang depending on the forces applied at specific angles.

For instance, most natural female breasts are not actually shaped like beach balls (despite popular artworks of many comic book and anime artists), but may better be described as resembling teardrops or bells, curvy or coned, heavy or sagging, athletic in build, sloped, rounded, shapely, east-west, petite, flat, or full. And gravity will certainly change those shapes as applied in different ways.

In *Foundational*, we can easily see the flattening effect the downward gravitational pull has on not only the woman's breasts, but her thighs, stomach, glutes, back, shoulders, arms, and hair.

1

2

3

4

UNUSUAL POSES
LEAN ON ME

Graphite, Color Pencil & Acrylic on Illustration Board
12 x 16 in.

Elongated or otherwise exaggerated figures can affect the overall mood or feel of a piece, giving the figurative work an extra touch of elegance or sense of divinity. Generally, short, stalky figures don't hold that same sense of otherworldly grandeur or sophistication as tall and graceful ones. Think of the different impressions one might get from Tolkein's Hobbits versus his Elves.

So when we're drawing the female figure, we can elongate primarily the limbs and neck, and then the torso and extremities, such as fingers and toes, for added grace. Many times, in photographs, women's legs or arms will appear shorter than they actually are in relation to the rest of their body, so as artists, we may take liberties in exggerating these features. Some women have long torsos and short legs or long legs and short torsos. We can play with proportions in the early sketching stages, not necessarily drawing things exactly as we see them. We can add a lot to a pose by pulling this or stretching that, and bringing our own style into the artistic equation.

1

2

3

4

UNUSUAL POSES
TENACITY

Graphite, Color Pencil & Acrylic on Wood Panel
16 x 20 in.

When tackling epic fantasy or science fiction concepts, such as mid-size paintings of warriors facing off against formidable beasts, for example, one must break down the elements into simple parts while simultaneously focusing on the overall composition. Otherwise, it can become overwhelming or much too tempting to get lost in the details. When shading and dropping in color, it can also be helpful to look at the value scheme across the entire piece, and how it all ties together visually in regard to the relationship between lights and darks. A consistent light source, varying textures, mostly soft edges with a few exceptions around focal points, and an ultimately complimentary color palette will tie the piece off with a nice bow, or—at the very least—make it something worth looking at.

On an aside, you might be asking yourself, why is this *Maidens & Monsters* piece included in a female figure drawing book, when our tenacious foreground heroine takes up less than even the bottom third of the active picture plane? Well, let's just say the dragon is also female.

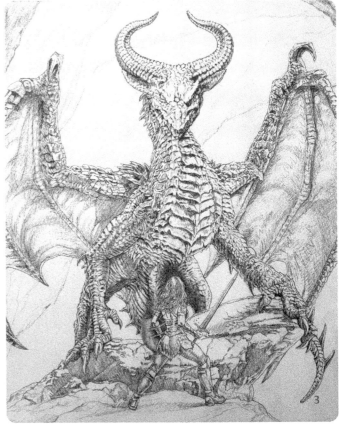

4

UNUSUAL POSES
THE SHAPE OF FIRE

Graphite, Color Pencil & Posca Marker on Toned Pastel
Paper
9 x 12 in.

As I've briefly touched on earlier in this volume, the way a "chiaroscuro drawing" is usually identified is when toned paper is used as a middle value with darker and lighter tones drawn or painted in. The root of this effect can be traced back to ancient woodcut prints. Typically the white areas in the prints came from the paper itself, and the rest was ink. This limited use of values has a long tradition that extends up to recent printmaking techniques. An alternative method is using white (marker or color pencil) first (3) for the highlights, the orange (or whatever color of toned paper you happen to be using) for the middle value, and darks (Tuscan Red and Burnt Ochre here in 4) sketched in last.

Inexpensive printing in the late 20th century also used a two-tone ("duo-tone") process with two inks, typically black and another color of a middle value, not unlike some of the other toned paper or ink images in this book, but sometimes it's just fun to switch it up and experiment with fire.

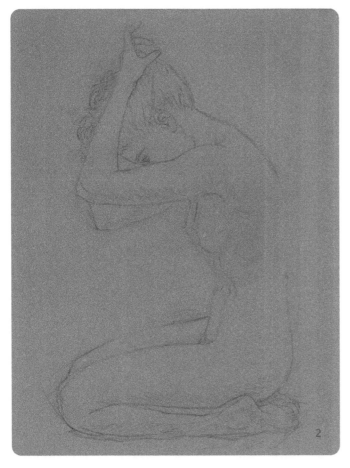

LIFE DRAWING STUDIES

B.C. HAILES

"Don't Look," 9 x 12 in., Color Pencil & Posca Marker on Toned Pastel Paper

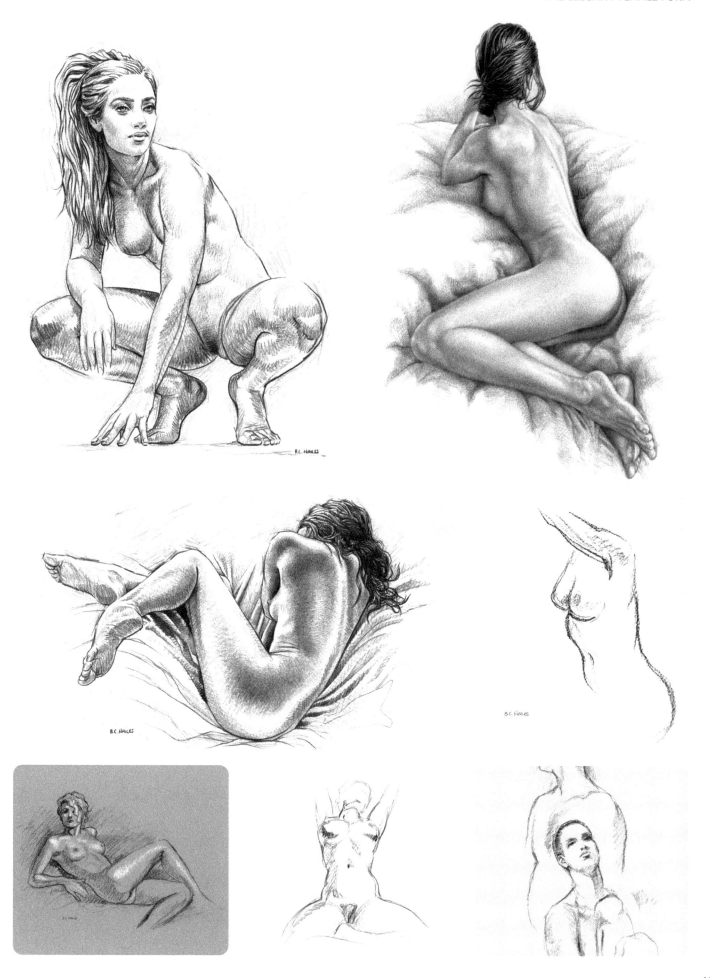

PORTRAITURE

B.C. HAILES

PORTRAITURE
GIRL IN THE SHADOW

Graphite, Color Pencil & Acrylic on Illustration Board
15 x 20 in.

For *Girl in the Shadow*, I stepped away from convention to follow a strange and exotic idea circling an Egyptian themed profile of a girl in black and white paint framed with gold standing or walking beside a backstaged dragon. A bold concept to be sure, but I feel it came together fairly well in the end.

Beginning with messy lines that shore up bit-by-bit throughout each stage, and using four separate reference photos during the initial drawing process—one for the face, a second for the girl's body, a third for her hair and a fourth of a bat wing—I tweak and change a few areas, careful to keep consistent lighting and form, as every 'Frankensteined' piece must feel like it belongs with the other.

I develop the girl's and dragon's casual stance and that slightly judgemental look in her eye, softening edges with the color pencils and even further with the acrylic on to the end . . . with gold. Lots of gold.

1

2

3

PORTRAITURE
CHRISTIE ON THE PILLOW

Graphite, Color Pencil & Acrylic on Illustration Board
12 x 16 in.

There are a few instances in a commercial artist's career where one must nail a likeness: commissions, movie posters, and portraits (especially when the subject happens to be your spouse). When working from photographs, it's important to choose those with not only great poses or expressions, but interesting shapes and compositions. The picture plane must compliment the subject, captivate the viewer, and contain a nice balance overall.

As many times before, we block out the major forms in subtle pencil (1), then carefully flesh out more of the details in contour, varying the line weight for good measure (2), and ultimately dropping in the chiaroscuro in color pencil and paint for value impact and finality (3). Many artists, particularly those with formal art school training in places like Florence, Paris or New York, are taught to begin with shadows and highlights rather than contour lines, and sometimes I will take that approach, but I generally find it more difficult to achieve a proper likeness that way.

1

2

PORTRAITURE

PORTRAIT OF AN ELEGANT WOMAN

Graphite, Color Pencil & Acrylic on Toned Paper
11 x 14 in.

Rendered for the front cover of this volume, *Portrait of an Elegant Woman* attempts to encapsulate the delicacy, dignity and grace of the human female form that I wanted to convey throughout every page of this work. That line between grandeur and charm, the sensual yet divinely dignified is a difficult one to walk for many figure artists, including myself. The juxtaposition of soft highlights and hard-lined shadows brings together the fine mixture of clinging or drooping drapery, locks of hair and the supple surface of flesh.

The thougtful pose inspired by Luigi Secchi's (1853-1921) brilliant sculpture, *La Meditazione*, supports the attempt, and the sketchy lines of the background (3) contrast nicely with the intentional, more tightly rendered figure. Finished off with a careful spread of acrylic in Payne's grey (4) to fill in some of the paper texture and give a smoother, glazed look, it all comes together.

4

PORTRAITURE
THE MAIDEN & THE DIRE WOLF

Graphite, Color Pencil & Acrylic on Wood Panel
18 x 24 in.

In steps 1 and 2, we work in the basic contour shapes softly in graphite, giving ourselves a gentle framework to develop later on. In step 3, we drop in the beginnings of chiaroscuro delicately identifying areas of light and shadow.

To help support the quiet, placid and relaxed mood of the pose, I'm careful to keep the edges soft as we move into the finish work and introduce watered down layers of paint, mindful of the direct light source from the upper right corner of the picture plane, and softly cast shadows down and to the left.

For color temperature on The Bather, I thought it might be nice to give the warmer tones to the girl and let the surroundings cool off into neutral shades of gray. So I focus most of the warm, mindful render work on the center of the figure and loosen up toward the outer edges and background area, giving the majority of thought to the woman standing in the towel, preparing for her bath.

PORTRAITURE
Taryn in Retro

Graphite, Color Pencil & Acrylic on Watercolor Board
12 x 16 in.

Watercolor can create beautiful washes that are a joy to brush onto paper. However, the medium can also be problematic. Because of its transparent nature, it's easy to lose control of it. Overworking and 'muddiness' can become an issue. Also, when it dries, it lightens and appears pale or faded. Often, a watercolor painting will look nice wet, but then when you return from lunch, the dried colors can seem dull. This is a quality that must be remembered when using it, and bumping the saturation up while it's wet will help. But that can be hard to do because while it's wet, it may appear too harsh.

That's mainly why I use acrylics as watercolor. When diluted with water into a transparent wash, acrylic paint looks very much like traditional watercolors. Each wash will dry true. No more surprise fading over the lunch hour. Also, you can apply many layers of washes into your acrylic painting without it 'muddying.' By allowing the washed area to dry and set, it becomes permanent. It won't re-hydrate when another wash of color is applied over it. This will keep the colors clean.

1

2

3

B.C. NAILES

4

PORTRAITURE
PRETTY AND PINK

Graphite, Color Pencil & Acrylic on Illustration Board
12 x 16 in.

Although I consider this an acrylic portrait painting, I still begin by sketching the outline of my subject in graphite and Tuscan Red color pencil (1-2). I focus on major features such as eyes, nose, mouth, neck and shoulders to ensure everything is in the correct proportions before painting. I flesh out the pencil detail in 2, then blend my colors to create a starting palette, beginning with skin tone. I'm using open acrylics here to slow drying time and make blending the primary colors easier. I start painting with a skin tone fill color before unleashing a variety of color on the image. I begin the process with larger brushes and then go back to add details and dimension with smaller ones. Remember, skin tones are never just one or two colors. I used mainly Cadmium Red, Pthalo Blue, Raw Umber and Yellow Ochre to create a realistic look. Once the base is somewhat completed it's time to move on to refining features. It's important to focus on blending your acrylics to create smooth transitions, include shadows and highlights, and make conscious choices about where to focus the details. You can also add a varnish to protect and enhance your portrait.

1

2

PORTRAITURE
MADE UP

Graphite, Color Pencil, Watercolor & Acrylic on Mixed
Media Board
12 x 16 in.

It would seem a flattering hairstyle and a chic jet-black
gown can just about do the work for you. With a slick
concept to prop up the design, veritably little effort is
required to turn a portrait into a stunning work of art that
practically paints itself. And, of course, a gorgeous model
underneath it all helps out too.

For *Made Up*, I wanted the waist of the gown to flare out into
abstract brush strokes and balance out the deep-set blacks
with some subtle blue/gray violets and bold splashes of
crimson. I frame the piece with more subtle scribbles of
gray around the edges so as to give a finished look but
without distracting from the star. The central composition
of the figure with those crisp edges of black against white
draws you in and leaves no question of focal point: the eyes,
lips, hair and bridled breasts under spaghetti-thin straps
leave the viewer somewhat if not unequivocally seduced.

1

2

3

LIFE DRAWING STUDIES

PORTRAITURE
GESTURES & 30–60 MINUTE SKETCHES

As shown across this spread, portraiture can take on a wide variety of applications and approaches. Portraits can be done on varied supports and using a plethora of media types. Their purpose can range from commission work, for someone to hang on a wall to magazine illustrations to gallery work to gifts, or simply for the personal pleasure and sense of accomplishment and progression in creating them. There can be no limit to the type of portraits—or figure drawings—one can make with a little time, a little patience, and that burning desire to leave your mark on the world and record the human presence. Drawing portraits from life, especially, can help one to appreciate others in a deeper, more meaningful way.

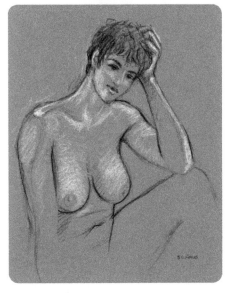

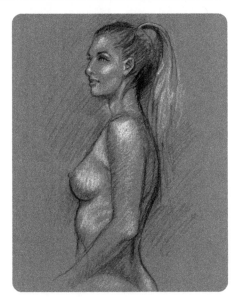

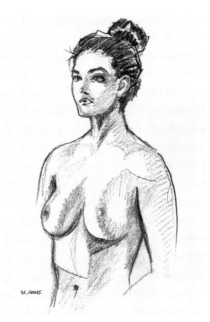

CONCLUSION

"Le Gentil" 12 x 9 in. Graphite & Color Pencil on Toned Paper

A final word . . .

Drawing the human figure is one of the most challenging, yet rewarding activities for an artist. The human figure is ever changing and no two body shapes are the same. This makes figure drawing a challenging skill that you can continue to develop over a lifetime. It can help one take a new interest in people; it presents the broadest opportunity for earning in many artistic endeavors; and it certainly progresses the skill level and work of students and professionals alike.

Of all the beautiful creations in this world, why the human figure? For one, the skill with which the figure is drawn is a telling standard for evaluating not only an artist's essential drawing ability, but his or her spirit and sensitivity as a human being. Author Nathan Goldstein wrote, "The psychological and philosophical implications embodied in human subjects, and the manner used to establish these implications through the act of drawing, can evince powerful expressive meanings. By losing ourselves in the intensity of a visual encounter with another's living nature we emerge with gain to *ourselves*—the satisfaction of better apprehending our own essential creative and human nature, as well as of achieving important insights about the people around us.

"Nor is an ability to draw the figure well of importance only to the representationally oriented student or professional artist. Something of the figure's spirit and form can be sensed as underlying many of the finest examples of abstract art, pottery, ornament, and architecture."[1] As the noted art historian Kenneth Clark has observed, "The nude does not simply represent the body, but relates it, by analogy, to all structures that have become part of our imaginative experience."[2]

"Some figure drawings have the power to affect and involve us deeply. The reasons why this is so have little to do with the artist's facility, objective accuracy, or choice of subject. Nor is time a factor, for some drawings have been with us for centuries, while others are very recent."[1] Whatever the reason for you personally, the struggle and practice required to improve and progress will most certainly be worth your while.

1 Nathan Goldstein, Figure Drawing: The Structure, Anatomy, and Expressive Design of Human Form (New Jersey: Prentice-Hall Books, 1981), p. 3.
2 Kenneth Clark, The Nude: A Study in Ideal Form (New York: Pantheon Books, Bollingen Foundation, 1953), p. 370.

A SPECIAL THANKS

To the Models & Other Contributors:

Contributors:
Christie Hailes
(Bookkeeper / Moral Support / Model)
Kent
(Model Session Host)
Jessica Jude Gilmore
(Model Session Host)
RT
(Model Session Host)
Bryce Cameron Liston
(Artist / Photographer)

Dancers/Models:
Artists of Ballet West
Artists of Cache Valley Civic Ballet
Artists of Central West Ballet
Artists of Ballet Centre
Artists of Ballroom Utah

Models:
Aeltie
Amber M
Anna
Arielle Miller
Becca B
Blake
Cami Allred
Caryn
Celeste
Chelsey Jimenez
Cosette R
Dane Halo
Debbie Higham Wood
Erin C
Genevieve Reynolds
Hailey J
Heather Rison
Hillary Sukhonos
Jessica
Katelynn
Kazia
Krystal W
Lauren Hunsaker
Lauren Paret
Lea Molina
Meagan Chadwick
Megan Golden
Michelle
Nicole
Polina Chernenko
Rebecca Erickson
Reese Riley
Ruth
Sarah Crowley
Sarah Manning
Taryn Lavery

* To purchase original artwork or prints appearing in this book
and other HailesArt titles, please visit: **HailesArt.com**

Other Titles by Brian C Hailes

Illustrated Novels
- Blink: An Illustrated Spy Thriller Novel
- Defender of Llyans
- McKenna (American Girl)
- McKenna, Ready to Fly (American Girl)
- Grace & Sylvie: Recipe For Family (American Girl)
- Avila (Available 2023!)

Graphic Novels / Comics
- Devil's Triangle: The Complete Graphic Novel
- Dragon's Gait
- KamiKazi
- Continuum (Arcana Comics)

Novellas
- The Isolated

Childrens Picture Books
- If I Were a Spaceman: A Rhyming Adventure Through the Cosmos
- Here, There Be Monsters
- Don't Go Near the Crocodile Ponds
- Skeleton Play

Anthologies
- Cresting the Sun: A Sci-fi / Fantasy Anthology Featuring 12 Award-Winning Short Stories
- Heroic: Tales of the Extraordinary

Non-Fiction
- Draw It With Me: The Dynamic Female Figure
- Draw It With Me: A Study of the Human Form
- Passion & Spirit: The Dance Quote Book with Artwork by B.C. Hailes

About the Author/Artist

Born at the base of the beautiful Wasatch Mountains, Brian began exploring and sketching the world—as most children do—at a very early age. He continued to pursue not only his artistic path through traditional schooling, higher education, and endless hours of practice, but also his love of storytelling. Utilizing his natural illustrative and creative design sense, he began writing and illustrating his own books through his teens and on into adulthood.

Intrigued by the Science Fiction and Fantasy genres, many of Hailes' projects reflect elements of the fantastic, but he also appreciates the beauty and elegance in fine art masterpieces by the likes of Bouguereau, Waterhouse, Alma-Tadema, and many others. He also feels a certain draw to the styles and ideals of the Pre-Raphaelite brotherhood of the mid-nineteenth century.

Hailes studied illustration and graphic design at Utah State University where he received his Bachelor of Fine Arts degree, as well as the Academy of Art University in San Francisco.

Having received several awards for his art from across the country, including Winner of the L. Ron Hubbard Illustrators of the Future contest out of Hollywood, his artwork has also been featured in the 2017-2023 editions of Infected By Art.

While continually pursuing progress and improvement by way of technique and application in his own works, he also keeps busy with design and commission work for a diverse clientele, including book covers, magazine illustration, corporate design as well as private commissions.

Hailes currently lives in Salt Lake City with his wife and four boys, where he continues to write, paint and draw regularly.

Other Titles Available from
Epic Edge Publishing

Illustrated Novels	Graphic Novels / Comics	Childrens Picture Books	Anthologies	Non-Fiction

Blink: An Illustrated Spy Thriller Novel
by Brian C Hailes

Devil's Triangle: The Complete Graphic Novel
by Brian C Hailes & Blake Casselman

If I Were a Spaceman: A Rhyming Adventure Through the Cosmos
by Brian C Hailes & Tithi Luadthong

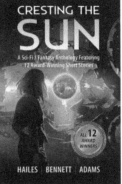

Cresting the Sun: A Sci-fi / Fantasy Anthology Featuring 12 Award-Winning Short Stories
by Brian C Hailes, Rick Bennett & Nicholas Adams

DIWM: A Study of the Human Form
by Brian C Hailes

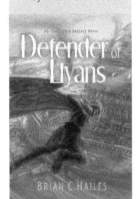

Defender of Llyans
by Brian C Hailes

Dragon's Gait
by Brian C Hailes

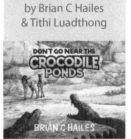

Here, There Be Monsters
by Brian C Hailes & Tithi Luadthong

Heroic: Tales of the Extraordinary
by Blake Casselman, David Farland, Michael Stackpole+

DIWM: The Dynamic Female Figure
by Brian C Hailes

Avila
(Available 2023!)
by Robert J Defendi & Brian C Hailes

KamiKazi
by John English & Brian C Hailes

Don't Go Near the Crocodile Ponds
by Brian C Hailes

Skeleton Play
by Brian C Hailes

Can We Be Friends?
by Edie New & Cindy Hailes

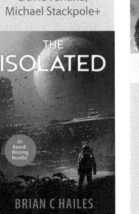

The Isolated
by Brian C Hailes

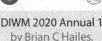

DIWM 2020 Annual 1
by Brian C Hailes, Heather Edwards & more

CPSIA information can be obtained
at www.ICGtesting.com
Printed in the USA
BVHW011806130323
660329BV00005B/126